CITIZEN SCIENCE PROJECTS

Bird Projects

BY CHRISTA KELLY

Kids Core
An Imprint of Abdo Publishing
abdobooks.com

abdobooks.com

Published by Abdo Publishing, a division of ABDO, PO Box 398166, Minneapolis, Minnesota 55439.

Printed in the United States of America, North Mankato, Minnesota.
102025
012026

Cover Photo: Shutterstock Images
Interior Photos: Bonnie Taylor Barry/Shutterstock Images, 4–5; Sophon Nawit/Shutterstock Images, 6; Shutterstock Images, 9, 15, 19 (top left, middle right), 19 (top right, bottom left, bottom right), 19 (middle left), 22–23, 26, 28 (top), 29 (bottom); Tatiana Buzmakova/Shutterstock Images, 10; Gordon Magee/Shutterstock Images, 12–13; Martin Pelanek/Shutterstock Images, 16; Malik Nalik/Shutterstock Images, 20; Bouke Atema/Shutterstock Images, 24; Steve Byland/Shutterstock Images, 28 (bottom); Bob L. Parker/Shutterstock Images, 29 (top)

Editors: Rebecca Higgins and Trudy Becker
Series Designer: Marley Richmond

Library of Congress Control Number: 2025939245

Publisher's Cataloging-in-Publication Data

Names: Kelly, Christa, author.
Title: Bird projects / by Christa Kelly
Description: Minneapolis, Minnesota: Abdo Publishing, 2026 | Series: Citizen science projects | Includes online resources and index.
Identifiers: ISBN 9781098298548 (lib. bdg.) | ISBN 9798384932345 (ebook)
Subjects: LCSH: Science projects--Juvenile literature. | Field experiments--Juvenile literature. | Birds--Juvenile literature. | Zoology --Experiments--Juvenile literature. | Ornithology--Juvenile literature. | Ecology--Experiments--Juvenile literature. | Ecological science--Juvenile literature.
Classification: DDC 507.8--dc23

CONTENTS

Male cardinals are bright red. Female cardinals are browner and harder to spot.

CHAPTER 1

Counting Birds

Leilani and her mom stepped outside. It was cold. The sun had not risen yet. But Leilani knew they had an important job to do. They were going to be part of the Christmas Bird Count.

This bird count has been running for more than 100 years.

People participating in the Christmas Bird Count may use binoculars to better see and identify birds.

Each winter, volunteers around the world go out into areas in their communities. The volunteers spend a few hours in each area looking for birds. These volunteers count each bird they see or hear. They keep track of what **species** they find.

Leilani and her mom started at their local park. Leilani looked around. There! She saw a yellow-brown bird with black-and-white wings. It was perched on a tree branch. She flipped through her book of local birds. It was an American goldfinch! Leilani's mom took a picture.

Leilani heard the soft sound of a birdcall. She looked around. She did not see any birds. But her mom said the call came from a cardinal. She wrote down the bird's name in a notebook.

They spent the next few hours looking. Leilani's mom kept track of the birds they found.

By the time they were ready to move on to the next park, they had found 24 species of birds. Leilani was excited. She knew their work would help researchers learn how to protect the birds in their neighborhood.

Citizen Science

Citizen scientists are regular people who help scientists with research projects.

Birdcalls

Birds make many different sounds. They make some sounds to attract mates. Birds make other sounds to scare away predators and other birds. Since different species make different sounds, people can use birdcalls to identify bird species.

Collecting information on birds helps scientists better understand the animals.

Citizen scientists often work with students and teachers. Each citizen scientist gathers information. Scientists then use the information in their studies.

Some citizen scientists take photos of the birds they are watching.

Some citizen scientists help with bird projects. They count how many birds are in a certain area. They track each species they see. They find and **monitor** birds' nests.

The **data** that citizen scientists collect helps scientists learn more about birds. The scientists see how the data changes over time. They figure out which species need protection. This keeps birds safe for the future. And it all starts with the hard work of citizen scientists.

Further Evidence

Look at the webpage below. Does it give any new evidence to support Chapter One?

Let's Go Birding

abdocorelibrary.com/bird-projects

Citizen scientists can count the number of baby birds in a nest.

CHAPTER 2

Bird-Watching Projects

There are many ways citizen scientists can help researchers learn more about birds. One way is by joining a bird-watching project. These projects generally involve counting birds or nests.

Scientists use counts to track bird behaviors. They also look for changes in **populations**. If there are fewer birds than in the past, scientists can work to protect the species from danger. Scientists might also discover that a bird species is behaving differently. They can look into why this change occurred.

Christmas Bird Count

One of the most famous bird-watching projects is the Christmas Bird Count. The Christmas Bird Count started in 1900. Each year, thousands of citizen scientists count birds and gather data. In 2024, citizen scientists counted birds in more than 20 different countries for the project.

More than 63,600 people in the United States participated in the 2024 Christmas Bird Count.

Christmas Bird Count volunteers are organized into groups based on where they live. These groups are called bird circles. Every group includes at least ten people. Each bird circle counts birds on a specific day.

During the 2024 Christmas Bird Count, a citizen scientist observed a mottled owl in Texas. It was the first time someone had tracked a mottled owl in the United States for the count.

The volunteers in a group can go anywhere in a 15-mile (24-km) circle chosen for them. They keep track of the number of birds they see from each species. They may count birds in several areas over the course of the day.

At the end of the day, each volunteer gives their data to a person called a compiler.

The compiler organizes the data and sends it to Audubon. This is the organization that runs the Christmas Bird Count. Audubon makes the data available to scientists. People who want to join the Christmas Bird Count can go to the Audubon website to look for a bird circle in their area.

How to Identify Birds

It can be hard to tell bird species apart. But bird-watchers can look for clues. Different species have different sizes, shapes, and colors. Bird-watchers can also use behavior to tell species apart. Different species make different sounds. They may also live in different places.

NestWatch

Some citizen scientists observe birds' nests with NestWatch. NestWatch is run by the Cornell Lab of **Ornithology**. The program teaches citizen scientists how to find and safely monitor birds' nests.

NestWatch explains how to check on nests without disturbing birds or attracting predators. Before citizen scientists can monitor nests, they must pass an online quiz. Those who pass are NestWatch certified and can look for a bird's nest to watch.

After finding a bird's nest, citizen scientists record the nest's location on the NestWatch website. They can also record what kind of area the nest is in. For example, they can note

Checking Nests Safely

Check the nest in the afternoon.

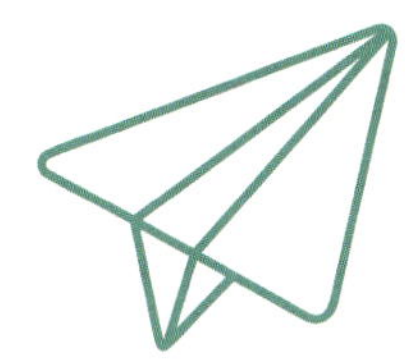

Do not approach the nest when baby birds are close to flying for the first time.

Make noise when approaching the nest.

Spend less than a minute at the nest.

Do not touch the eggs or the nest.

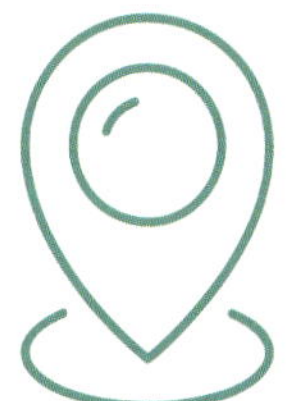

Take a different path to and from the nest.

When checking on a bird's nest, citizen scientists should follow some rules so that they do not put birds in danger.

whether the nest is in a **bird box** or in a tree. Then citizen scientists start collecting data on the nest.

NestWatch recommends that citizen scientists check the nest every three to four days. People take notes during each visit. They write down which bird species lives in the nest. Citizen scientists record how many eggs they see. They also record the number of baby birds in the nest. This information helps scientists understand bird life patterns. It also helps them measure how many birds live in an area.

Each time citizen scientists visit nests, they should write down what they see.

Chan Robbins was a biologist who studied birds. He believed that the Christmas Bird Count was important. Robbins said:

> If we had not had a Christmas Bird Count in those early years, we would not have as strong an understanding of long-term bird **trends**. Many of these changes take place **gradually**.

Source: "'Tis the Season for the Christmas Bird Count." *US Fish & Wildlife Service*, n.d., fws.gov. Accessed 12 Mar. 2025.

Point of View

What is the speaker's point of view? What is your point of view? Write a short essay about how they are similar and different.

Canada geese are one of the bird species that get banded.

Birdbanding

Some bird projects use birdbanding to learn more about birds. Birdbanding is a process in which a small band is placed on a bird's leg. The band has a code written on it. This allows scientists to tell individual birds apart and track them over time.

Only people trained in birdbanding should do it. Otherwise, the people and the birds could get hurt.

Birdbanders generally catch birds in nets. They carefully take each bird out of the net and record the species and size. Then they place a band around the bird's leg. Finally, they release the bird. The process takes only a few minutes.

Finding Bands

Some research organizations let citizen scientists help with birdbanding. But most citizen scientists cannot band birds. People must have a permit to put bands on birds. This makes sure they know how to band birds correctly and do not harm birds. But citizen scientists can still support birdbanding projects.

One way citizen scientists can help birdbanders is by letting researchers know when they see a banded bird. This gives scientists data about where the birds are.

When a person sees a banded bird, they should record as much information as possible.

Barbara Patterson

Barbara Patterson was a citizen scientist. She spent more than 20 years birdbanding songbirds. She collected data from more than 30,000 birds. Her data is still used today to track changes in bird activity.

Citizen scientists who see a banded bird should record what they see so scientists can learn more about the bird.

They should write down the date the bird was seen and the bird's location. Then they should note where the band is on the bird, what the band says, the color of the band, and the color of the writing.

Once a person has recorded information about a banded bird, they can submit the information to the North American Bird Banding Program. This organization keeps track of banded birds. Program workers can get this information to scientists.

Citizen scientists help researchers gather data. Then scientists can learn more about birds and their behavior. Citizen science projects help protect birds.

Explore Online

Look at the website below. Does it give any new information about North American birds?

Bird Guide

abdocorelibrary.com/bird-projects

Science Projects

Citizen scientists should be familiar with their area's local birds.

Volunteers who monitor nests may need to be NestWatch certified and able to access the NestWatch website.

Volunteers might need a birdbanding license.

Citizen scientists may need access to the North American Bird Banding Program website.

Glossary

bird box
a box made by people that birds can live in

data
information

gradually
slowly over time

monitor
to watch or keep track of

ornithology
the study of birds

populations
the numbers of individuals in certain areas

species
a group of similar living things that can produce young with one another

trends
patterns of change

Online Resources

To learn more about bird projects, visit our free resource websites below.

Visit **abdocorelibrary.com** or scan this QR code for free Common Core resources for teachers and students, including vetted activities, multimedia, and booklinks, for deeper subject comprehension.

Visit **abdobooklinks.com** or scan this QR code for free additional online weblinks for further learning. These links are routinely monitored and updated to provide the most current information available.

Learn More

Hoare, Ben. *An Anthology of Exquisite Birds.* DK, 2024.

Mayntz, Melissa. *Birds for Kids.* Sourcebooks, 2024.

Perdew, Laura. *Spotting Birds.* Abdo, 2026.

Index

About the Author

Christa Kelly is an author and editor from Minnesota. She lives with her wife and their two cats, Casey and Honey Cheddar.